Japanese Reader Collection Volume 6: Yuki Onna

+ Anchin & Kiyohime

The Easy Way to Read Japanese Folklore, Tales, and Stories

Clay & Yumi Boutwell

Copyright © 2017-2021 Kotoba Books
www.TheJapanShop.com
www.TheJapanesePage.com
www.MakotoPlus.com

All rights reserved.

Makoto Monthly E-Zine for Learners of Japanese

Japanese lessons and stories with sound files.

It's only a few bucks a month!

https://www.thejapanesepage.com/makoto

You'll get:
Download the Latest Makoto Issue | Read 3 Full Back Issues Online | Reusable TheJapanShop.com Coupon | Monthly Freebies

INTRODUCTION

The key to learning vocabulary is, quite simply, reading. Not only are you more likely to pick up words that interest you, but you also learn them **in context**. The **Japanese Reader Collection Series** goes one step further by adding **MP3s of the Japanese**. Improve your **listening comprehension** while building your **vocabulary, kanji,** and **reading skills**.

FORMAT OF THIS READER

By choosing **short stories**, the intimidation factor is greatly reduced. Not only that, but we divide the story up into tiny, easy-to-swallow segments with complete explanations to give you confidence as you read **real Japanese** page by page.

The stories are selected to represent certain key aspects Japanese culture. The tales, characters, and even moral lessons are often found in Japanese conversation, movies, and manga. Knowing these stories will go well beyond simply improving your vocabulary. **It will help you understand Japanese culture as well.**

www.TheJapanShop.com

This book is designed so that both those fairly new to Japanese and those in the intermediate stages can equally get value out of it. We recommend learning hiragana first, but we are also including rōmaji in the definitions so you can be sure you are reading with the correct pronunciation. For a quick two-week crash course for mastering hiragana, please see our book: Hiragana, the Basics of Japanese.

This book has two complete stories with several versions of each.

- **Line-by-line:** Read the story broken down line-by-line with every vocabulary word defined and explained.

- **Grammatical Notes:** In this section, we go through important grammatical patterns found in the story and attempt to explain them in plain English. The grammar icon 文法 found in the line-by-line definitions indicates there is a note for that word or phrase.

- **Full Japanese with Furigana:** Read the full story in *real* Japanese. Every kanji has furigana above it. Furigana is the small hiragana above kanji so even beginners can work through the text.

- **English Version:** Lastly, we are including a simple English translation. This should be avoided until you are sure you understand the story or find it too difficult to figure out on your own.

You may want to try to read the story in Japanese with furigana first. Or if you are a beginner, it may be better to go through the line-by-line story before attempting the full Japanese text. Any way you do it, **this book offers several** ways to read, listen, and learn.

Kanji in Focus: This is a new section to help with that incredibly difficult task of learning those Chinese characters. We take many of the kanji found in the story and present the readings, meaning(s), and an example sentence:

姫 princess

READINGS	チキ; ひめ; ひめ
MEANING	princess
EXAMPLE	一姫二太郎 (いちひめにたろう) [Japanese saying] It's best to have a baby girl first, then a boy.

MP3s: Included at no extra charge are two MP3s of each story. One is read at the normal speed and the other at a slow, easy-to-follow pace. If the MP3s were not included when you purchased this book, please see the last page for a download link. If you have ANY trouble downloading, please email us at help@thejapanshop.com.

ABOUT YUKI ONNA

In Japanese folklore, the Yuki Onna (literally, "snow woman") is a spirit or *yōkai* that appears to travelers on snowy nights. She appears as a beautiful—but pale—woman who often leads men astray, floating and never leaving footprints in the snow.

The Wikipedia page on Yuki Onna has several tales from different Japanese regions:
https://en.wikipedia.org/wiki/Yuki-onna

ABOUT ANCHIN & KIYOHIME

This is an ancient tale—over a thousand years old. A beautiful young woman falls madly in love with a traveling priest named Anchin. Unfortunately, her constant demands for his love turns him against her. In doing so, she changes...into something else entirely.

Like Yuki Onna, this is a traditional Japanese tale of horror.

ABOUT CLAY & YUMI

Yumi was a popular radio DJ in Japan for over ten years. She has extensive training in standard Japanese pronunciation which makes her perfect for creating these language instructional audio files.

Clay has been a passionate learner of Japanese for twenty years now. He started his free language learning website, www.TheJapanesePage.com, way back in 1999 as a way to help other learners of Japanese as well as himself.

In 2002, he and Yumi opened www.TheJapanShop.com as a way to help students of Japanese get hard-to-find Japanese books.

Yumi and I are **very grateful** for your purchase and we truly hope this book will help you improve your Japanese. **We love our customers and don't take a single one of you for granted.** If you have any questions about this book or Japanese in general, I invite you to contact me below by email or on social media.

Japanese Reader Collection Volume 6: Yuki Onna

Clay & Yumi Boutwell (and Makoto & Megumi)
clay@thejapanshop.com
@theJapanShop
www.facebook.com/JapaneseReader
http://www.TheJapanShop.com
http://www.TheJapanesePage.com

P.S. Please see the last page of the book to find the download link for the MP3s of these stories free of charge.

CONTENTS

Table of Contents

Makoto Monthly E-Zine for Learners of Japanese ii

INTRODUCTION iii

Yuki Onna, the Snow Woman with Definitions 10

Yuki Onna, the Snow Woman in Japanese 42

Yuki Onna English Summary 49

LAFCADIO HEARN'S VERSION 49

Anchin and Kiyohime with Definitions 52

Anchin and Kiyohime in Japanese 75

Anchin and Kiyohime in English 79

Kanji in Focus 81

DOWNLOAD LINK 87

ゆきおんな
雪女

Yuki Onna (Snow Woman) is a traditional Japanese folktale of a spirit or *yōkai* who appears on snowy nights in a white kimono and even whiter skin.

She is beautiful, but deadly, leading unsuspecting travellers astray or killing them outright. In our story, she is both deadly and compassionate.

We are using the names of the father and son (Mosaku and Minokichi) from Lafcadio Hearn's famous version of the legend.

www.TheJapanShop.com

Story One:

Yuki Onna, the Snow Woman with Definitions

Story Read Slowly

Story Read Normal Speed

 Scan the QR codes for instant and FREE access to audio recordings

昔、寒い国に茂作と美濃吉という、きこりの親子が住んでいました。

むかし a long time ago
寒い cold
国 nation; country
に in (a cold country)
茂作 Mosaku [the father's name]
と and
美濃吉 [the son's name]
という such as (names); were so (named)
きこり woodcutter; lumberjack
親子 parent and child
きこりの親子 parent and child woodcutters
が [particle that often marks the subject]
住んでいました lived

ある寒い雪の日、二人は山へ行って木を切っていましたが、いつのまにか、すっかり吹雪になってしまいました。

ある one; some...
寒い cold
雪 snow
日 day
雪の日 (one cold) snowy day
二人 the two (father and son)
は [topic marker]
山 mountain
山へ行って went to the mountain
木 tree
を [direct object marker]
切っていました cut (trees)
が but; however
いつのまにか suddenly; all of the sudden
すっかり completely; thoroughly
吹雪 blizzard
になってしまいました became

仕方（しかた）なく、二人（ふたり）は近（ちか）くにあった小（ちい）さな小屋（こや）に泊（と）まって、吹雪（ふぶき）がおさまるのを待（ま）っていましたが、いつまでたってもおさまりません。

仕方なく reluctantly; without a choice
近くにあった close; nearby (cabin) [近くに (close by) + あった ((small cabin) was there; from ある (to exist)); there exists nearby...]
小さな小屋 a small cabin
に泊まって stayed there
吹雪 blizzard; snow storm
が [particle that usually marks the subject]
おさまる to calm down; lessen
の nominalizes phrases (the act of the blizzard lessening) [The の takes the preceding words and makes them into a noun phrase. こと is another nominalizer and is often interchangeable with の. くすりを飲むのは大事です。 *kusuri wo nomu no wa daiji desu.* Taking medicine is important.]
待っていました wait for (the blizzard to lessen)
が but; however [This is another common use for が]
いつまでたっても no matter how long waited
おさまりません wouldn't lessen

とうとう、夜になってしまい、二人はすっかり眠り込んでしまいました。

とうとう finally; at last
夜になってしまい became night [the しまい shows completeness.]
二人 the two
すっかり completely
眠り込んでしまいました fell asleep

Japanese Reader Collection Volume 6: Yuki Onna

どのくらい時間(じかん)がたったでしょうか。むすこの美濃吉(みのきち)は、あまりの寒(さむ)さに目(め)をさましました。

どのくらい how ever long
時間がたった time passed
どのくらい時間がたったでしょうか how much time passed? (is unknowable)
むすこ son
美濃吉 Minokichi (son's name)
むすこの美濃吉 Minokichi, the son
あまり too much; fullness; excess
の寒さに by the degree of cold (too much coldness)
目をさましました (he) awoke [literally, "(his) eyes awoke"]

外は、まだ吹雪で、風がごーごーとなっています。
　小屋の戸がはずれて外の雪が吹き込んでいます。

外 outside
まだ still
吹雪 blizzard; snowstorm
で and
風 wind
ごーごー rumbling (the effect of wind blowing hard)
となっています was happening; was becoming
小屋 cabin
戸 door
はずれて opened [literally, get off; (door) got out of place]
外の the outside…
雪 snow
吹き込んでいます blew in [吹く *fuku* (to blow) + 込む *komu* (to go into; to put into)]

すると、そのとき、真っ白な着物を着た、色の白い美しい女がすーっと中に入ってきました。

すると and then...; upon doing so...
そのとき at that time; just then
真っ白な completely white [The 真っ means "completely" or "purely." 真っ黒 *makkuro* (completely black); 真っ暗 *makkura* (completely dark; pitch dark); 真っ最中 *massaichuu* (in the midst; during)]
着物 kimono
着物を着た wore a kimono
色の the color of...
白い white
美しい beautiful
女 woman
すーっと *[effect of the woman gliding inside.]*
中に into the inside
入ってきました came inside

女は、お父さんの茂作の上にかがむと、ふーっと白い息を吹きかけました。

お父さん father
茂作 Mosaku
お父さんの茂作 Mosaku, the father
上に on top of; above
かがむと upon stooping over; upon leaning over [The と adds "upon doing this" to the meaning.]
ふーっと [effect of her breathing out]
白い息 white breath
吹きかけました blew out

すると、あっという間にお父さんの体は、白くこおりついて、眠ったまま死んでしまいました。

すると upon doing so
あっという間に just like that; in an instant [Literally, in the time it takes to say "ah." This is a common and useful phrase for describing when something happens quickly.]
お父さん father
体 body
白く white
こおりついて iced over
眠ったまま while sleeping; during sleep [〜まま *mama* is a useful particle that adds the meaning of "as it is." そのまま *sono mama* (as is; (leave it) just like that)]
死んでしまいました died

美濃吉は、心の中で「雪女だ!」と思いました。雪の降る寒い夜に、人を凍え死にさせるという恐ろしい雪女です。

心の中で within his heart (without speaking)
「」 —quotation marks (for what he is thinking)
雪女 *yuki onna*—the snow woman [雪女 literally means "snow woman." 雪男 *yuki otoko* is the word for "the Abominable Snowman" or the "Yeti."]
と思いました he thought [This can also mean "he remembered" but in this case, these were his thoughts.]
雪の降る falling snow
寒い夜に on a cold evening
人を凍え死にさせる to freeze someone to death
という such a; such as
恐ろしい scary; frightening

美濃吉は、逃げようと思いましたが、体が動きません。雪女は、美濃吉に近づいて、その顔をじっとのぞきこんでいましたが、こう言いました。

逃げよう escape! Get out of here
と思いましたが thought to (escape) but...
体 body
が [particle that usually marks the subject]
動きません didn't move
に近づいて came close
その顔 that face
じっと motionlessly; fixedly
のぞきこんでいましたが gazed at, but...
こう言いました said this...

「お前は、美しい顔をしている。まだ若いし、助けてあげよう。

お前は as for you
美しい顔 beautiful face; lovely face
している sporting; having (a lovely face)
美しい顔をしている having a lovely face
まだ still
若い young
し as well [notes one of several reasons (you are still young)]
助けてあげよう I'll help you out

ただし、今夜のことは、けっして誰にも話してはいけない。」

ただし however; but
今夜 this evening
今夜のこと what occurred this evening [こと literally means "thing" and can be thought of as "the thing of …": the thing of tonight (what happened tonight); koto isn't used for tangible things. It is usually used of things that are known or spoken about but cannot actually be touched: henna koto wo iu—to say something strange. If you have a tangible thing, use もの mono: henna mono wo mita—to see a strange thing. Sometimes both koto and mono are interchangeable.]
けっして by no means; never
誰にも to no one [followed by a negative verb form]
話してはいけない must not be spoken [~ikenai means "must not do" and it follows what must not be done (speak about her).]

雪女は、静かに雪の中に消えていきました。美濃吉は、そのまま気を失ってしまいました。

静かに quietly
雪の中に into the snow
消えていきました disappeared
そのまま just like that; without change
気を失ってしまいました lost consciousness; fainted

朝、目が覚めると、お父さんは隣で死んでいました。美濃吉は、ひとりで暮らすようになりましたが、雪女の話は、誰にもしませんでした。

朝 morning
目が覚めると upon waking up
お父さん the father
隣で beside; next to
死んでいました was dead
ひとりで all alone; by himself
暮らす to live; to make a living
ようになりました became like that (he lived alone)
が but; however
雪女の話 the story of Yuki Onna
誰にも to no one
しませんでした didn't (tell about Yuki Onna)

それから、一年たったある冬の日、美濃吉の家に美しい女がやってきて、こう言いました。

それから since then
一年たった one year passed
ある冬の日 one winter day
美濃吉の家に to Minokichi's house
美しい女 a beautiful woman
やってきて came along; showed up
こう言いました said the following

「雪で困っています。どうか一晩だけ泊めてください。」

雪で with snow
困っています troubled (with snow)
どうか please; somehow
一晩 one night
だけ only
泊めてください please let (me) to stay

美濃吉は、かわいそうに思い、泊めてあげました。その女は、お雪という名でした。話しているうちに、美濃吉は、お雪がすっかり気に入ってしまい、夫婦になることにしました。

かわいそうに pitying; feeling sorry for
思い (pitying) thoughts
泊めてあげました allowed (her) to stay
その女 that woman
お雪 Oyuki (her name) [Notice 雪 *yuki* (snow) is part of her name.]
という名でした was called; her name was…
話しているうちに while talking
すっかり completely; thoroughly
気に入ってしまい pleased with; suited for; liked
夫婦になる become husband and wife
ことにしました was decided to (become husband and wife)

何年かたち、二人の間にかわいい子供も生まれました。

何年かたち several years later [*nan nen* (how many years) + *ka* ([uncertainty]) + *tachi* (to pass; to lapse); the か here shows uncertainty: how many years passed?]
二人の間に between the two; among the two
かわいい cute
子供 child
も also
生まれました was born

ある冬の夜、美濃吉は、そばに座っているお雪の横顔を見ながら、ふと昔のことを思い出しました。

ある冬 one winter [Like か, ある is used to show uncertainty or inexactitude: あるひ aru hi (one day); ある人 aru hito (some person)]
冬の夜 winter evening
そばに next to
座っている sat; sitting
お雪 Oyuki (wife's name)
の横顔 the side of (her) face
見ながら while looking at
ふと unexpectedly; suddenly; casually
昔のこと something that happened long ago [Again, こと koto (thing) is used with intangible things like memories.]
思い出しました remembered

「お雪、わしはお前によく似た美しい女に会ったことがある。」

わし I [わし is usually used by older and old-fashioned men. The most common first-person pronoun is わたし watashi which can be used by men and women.]
お前 you
によく似た looked very much like (you)
美しい女 a beautiful woman
に会ったことがある I met (her) [ことがある koto ga aru is a common construction for "(I) have done …" Just add it to the plain past form of a verb. 食べたことがある tabeta koto ga aru. (I've) eaten that before. 見たことがある。 mita koto ga aru. (I've) seen that before (movie; bird; person)]

お雪は、顔を上げて美濃吉の顔を見てたずねました。「どこでその人にあったのですか？」

顔を上げて raised (her) face; looked up
顔を見て looked at (his) face
たずねました asked
どこで where at
その人 that person
にあった met
のですか？ [question ender wanting an explanation; のです or のだ or the abbreviated forms んです or んだ are used when giving or asking for an explanation for something. The reason is that… The fact is that…]

「あれは、何年も前のことだ。山で吹雪にあって、一晩小屋に泊まったことがあるのだ。

あれは as for that
何年も several years; many years
前のこと something that happened in the past
だ [simple past copula]
山で in the mountains; at the mountain
吹雪 blizzard; snowstorm
にあって met (a snowstorm)
一晩 one evening
小屋に in a cabin
泊まったことがある it happened (we) stayed (in the cabin)

そのとき、雪女にあったんだ。そうだ、お前はその雪女にそっくりだ。」

　すると、お雪は、悲しそうな顔で、こう言いました。

そのとき at that time
雪女 Yuki Onna; Snow Woman
にあったんだ (we) met
そうだ ah, yes
お前 you
その雪女 that Snow Woman
にそっくり just like; the spitting image
だ [past simple copula]
すると upon doing that; after that
悲しそうな a sad look; sadly [〜そう ~sō means "like" or "looks like" or "feels like." It shows the speaker's feeling about what he or she is observing: samusō (looks cold); oishisō (looks delicious)]
顔 face
で with (a sad face)
こう言いました said like this

「どうして話してしまったのですか。雪女に会ったことは、誰にも言ってはいけないといったではありませんか。」

お雪は、すっと立ち上がりました。

どうして why
話してしまった said [the *shimatta* indicates completion, but also often, as in this case, completion with regret.]
のですか [question asking for explanation]
に会ったことは (your) meeting with (her)
誰にも to no one [followed by a negative verb]
言ってはいけない not allowed to say
といった said [the と indicates the previous is a quote]
ではありませんか didn't (I warn you not to say)
お雪 Oyuki (her name)
は [topic particle]
すっと straight away; quickly; all of a sudden
立ち上がりました stood up; got up

「どうして、知っているんだ。お雪。まさか、お前は・・・」

お雪は、あのときの雪女に変わっていました。

どうして why; how
知っているんだ (did you) know
まさか wait, it can't be…; by no means!; certainly not…
お前は you
あのときの that time
雪女に変わっていました changed into the Snow Woman

「そうです。私(わたし)は、あのときの雪女(ゆきおんな)です。もうあなたと一緒(いっしょ)にくらすことは出来(でき)ません。」

そうです yes, that's right.
私は I am...
あのときの雪女 the Snow Woman from back then
もう no more
あなたと with you
一緒に together
くらすことは出来ません cannot live (with you)

そして、静かに戸をあけて、雪の中に消えていきました。「待ってくれ、お雪、ゆるしてくれ。」
　雪の中から、お雪の声だけが聞こえてきました。

そして and then
静かに quietly
戸をあけて open the door and...
雪の中に into the snow
消えていきました disappeared
待ってくれ wait please! [〜くれ is often used when asking for favors: "give me" "please do this for me"]
ゆるしてくれ forgive me!
雪の中から from (inside) the snow
お雪の声 Oyuki's voice
だけ only; just
聞こえてきました was able to hear

「あなたのことは、忘れません。子供のことを頼みます。さようなら。」

あなたのことは regarding you [こと koto means "thing" or "matter" and is used for intangible things. In this case, it isn't "you" (something tangible), but all the intangible matters regarding "you": memories; hopes; plans for the future; etc.]
忘れません won't forget
子供のこと regarding the children's wellbeing
頼みます to entrust care to [頼む *tanomu* usually means "to request" or "to ask," but it is also often used when leaving something in the care of someone else. Your boss might say, "Tanomu!" as he leaves you with a pile of papers to go through.]
さようなら goodbye [The most common way to say "bye" in Japanese is バイ *bai* (bye) or またね *mata ne* (see you again). さようなら is mostly used when parting for a long time.]

美濃吉は、外に飛び出し、雪の中を探しましたが、お雪の姿はどこにも見当たりませんでした。

外に to the outside
飛び出し jumped out into
雪の中 in the snow
探しましたが searched but…
お雪の姿 Oyuki's figure
どこにも nowhere
見当たりませんでした wasn't found [Japanese makes it fairly easy to create compound verbs. This one combines 見る *miru* (to see) with 当たり *atari* (to hit; to succeed). When you look around and find what you are looking for, you 見当たります. But if you don't, you 見当たりません. The でした makes it past tense.]

ただ、白い雪が降り続くばかりでした。

おしまい。

ただ nothing but; only; merely; simply
白い雪 white snow
降り続く (snow) continued to fall [The snow isn't just falling, but it continues to fall: 降る *furu* (to fall (rain, hail, snow…)) + 続く (to continue)]
ばかり only; nothing but; mostly
おしまい the end

STORY ONE:
雪女
<small>ゆきおんな</small>

Yuki Onna, the Snow Woman in Japanese

　昔、寒い国に茂作と美濃吉という、きこりの親子が住んでいました。

　ある寒い雪の日、二人は山へ行って木を切っていましたが、いつのまにか、すっかり吹雪になってしまいました。

　仕方なく、二人は近くにあった小さな小屋に泊まって、吹雪がおさまるのを待っていましたが、いつまでたってもおさまりません。とうとう、夜になってしまい、二人はすっかり眠り込んでしまいました。

どのくらい時間がたったでしょうか。むすこの美濃吉は、あまりの寒さに目をさましました。外は、まだ吹雪で、風がごーごーとなっています。

小屋の戸がはずれて外の雪が吹き込んでいます。すると、そのとき、真っ白な着物を着た、色の白い美しい女がすーっと中に入ってきました。

女は、お父さんの茂作の上にかがむと、ふーっと白い息を吹きかけました。すると、あっという間にお父さんの体は、白くこおりついて、眠ったまま死んでしまいました。

美濃吉は、心の中で「雪女だ！」と思いました。雪の降る寒い夜に、人を凍え死にさせるという恐ろしい

雪女です。

　美濃吉は、逃げようと思いましたが、体が動きません。雪女は、美濃吉に近づいて、その顔をじっとのぞきこんでいましたが、こう言いました。

　「お前は、美しい顔をしている。まだ若いし、助けてあげよう。ただし、今夜のことは、けっして誰にも話してはいけない。」

　雪女は、静かに雪の中に消えていきました。美濃吉は、そのまま気を失ってしまいました。朝、目が覚めると、お父さんは隣で死んでいました。美濃吉は、ひとりで暮らすようになりましたが、雪女の話は、誰にもしませんでした。

　それから、一年たったある冬の

日、美濃吉の家に美しい女がやってきて、こう言いました。

「雪で困っています。どうか一晩だけ泊めてください。」

美濃吉は、かわいそうに思い、泊めてあげました。その女は、お雪という名でした。話しているうちに、美濃吉は、お雪がすっかり気に入ってしまい、夫婦になることにしました。

何年かたち、二人の間にかわいい子供も生まれました。

ある冬の夜、美濃吉は、そばに座っているお雪の横顔を見ながら、ふと昔のことを思い出しました。

「お雪、わしはお前によく似た美しい女に会ったことがある。」

お雪は、顔を上げて美濃吉の顔を見てたずねました。
　「どこでその人にあったのですか？」
　「あれは、何年も前のことだ。山で吹雪にあって、一晩小屋に泊まったことがあるのだ。そのとき、雪女にあったんだ。そうだ、お前はその雪女にそっくりだ。」
　すると、お雪は、悲しそうな顔で、こう言いました。
　「どうして話してしまったのですか。雪女に会ったことは、誰にも言ってはいけないといったではありませんか。」
　お雪は、すっと立ち上がりました。
　「どうして、知っているんだ。お

雪。まさか、お前は・・・」

お雪は、あのときの雪女に変わっていました。

「そうです。私は、あのときの雪女です。もうあなたと一緒にくらすことは出来ません。」

そして、静かに戸をあけて、雪の中に消えていきました。「待ってくれ、お雪、ゆるしてくれ。」

雪の中から、お雪の声だけが聞こえてきました。

「あなたのことは、忘れません。子供のことを頼みます。さようなら。」

美濃吉は、外に飛び出し、雪の中を探しましたが、お雪の姿はどこにも見当たりませんでした。ただ、白い雪が降り続くばかりでした。

おしまい。

STORY ONE:

Yuki Onna English Summary
LAFCADIO HEARN'S VERSION

Please try to tackle the Japanese first and use this only as needed.

  A long time ago, there lived two woodcutters, Minokichi and Mosaku. Minokichi was young and Mosaku was very old.
  One winter day, they could not come back home because of a snowstorm. They found a hut in the mountain and decided to sleep there. On this particular evening, Mosaku woke up and found a beautiful lady with white clothes. She breathed on old Mosaku and he was frozen to death.
  She then approached Minokichi to breathe on him, but stared at him for a while, and said, "I thought I was going to kill you, the same as that old man, but I will not, because you are young and beautiful. You must not tell anyone about this incident. If you tell anyone about me, I will kill you."
  Several years later, Minokichi met a beautiful young lady, named Oyuki (yuki = "snow") and married her. She was a good wife. Minokichi and Oyuki had several children and lived happily for many years. Mysteriously, she did not age.
  One night, after the children were asleep, Minokichi said to Oyuki: "Whenever I see you, I am reminded of a mysterious incident that happened to me. When I was young, I met a beautiful young lady like you. I do not know if it was a dream or if she was a Yuki-onna..."
  After finishing his story, Oyuki suddenly stood up, and said "That woman you met was me! I told you that I would kill you if you ever told anyone about that incident. However, I can't kill you because of our children. Take care of our children..." Then she

melted and disappeared. No one saw her again.

Story Two:
あん陳（ちん）と清姫（きよひめ）

Another deadly woman, but this time, she's a serpent.

A traveling priest. A beautiful daughter. He makes promises he doesn't keep. A lie he told leads to a tragic end.

あん陳と清姫
あんちん きよひめ

Anchin and Kiyohime with Definitions

Story Read Slowly

Story Read Normal Speed

Scan the QR codes for instant and FREE access to audio recordings

今(いま)から千年(せんねん)ほど昔(むかし)のこと。

今から from now [Literally, "now from." から *kara* is a partidcle used to indicate a starting place in time or space. ここから *koko kara* (from here); あしたから *ashita kara* (from tomorrow). In this case, it is going back in time. From now back a thousand years…]

千年 thousand years

ほど approximately; around; about [This particle indicates a degree to which something does something. それほど *sore hodo* (to that extent)]

昔 long time ago

こと thing; matter; event; occurrence; incident

昔のこと something occurred a long time ago [こと literally means "thing" and can be thought of as "the thing of …": the thing of a long time ago (what happened a long time ago); koto isn't used for tangible things. It is usually used for things that are known or spoken about but cannot actually be touched: へんなことを言(い)う (to say something strange). If you have a tangible thing, use もの: へんなものを見(み)た (To see a strange thing). Sometimes *koto* and *mono* are interchangeable.]

53

あるところに「あん珍」という名の若い山伏がいました。

あるところに in a certain place [ある shows uncertainty: ある日 (one day); ある人 (some person)]

あん珍 Anchin [the young priest's name]

という such a (name); called thus

名 name

若い young

山伏 mountain priest; itinerant Buddhist monk

「あん珍」という名の若い山伏 A young mountain priest named "Anchin"

いました there lived; there existed

山伏(やまぶし)というのは、山(やま)に住(す)んで仏教(ぶっきょう)の修行(しゅぎょう)をする人(ひと)です。

というのは regarding...; such a thing as...
山伏というのは regarding a yamabushi...
山に on a mountain; in the mountains
住んで lived (on the mountain and...) [The plain form is 住(す)む. This is the ~*te* form which is used with verbs and adjectives to link sentences or clauses. A good way to "translate" it would be "and" or "-ing."]
仏教 Buddhism
修行 training; practice; study
仏教の修行 Buddhist training
する人 a person who did (Buddhist training) [A verb behind a noun is a way to show the action that the noun does: 食(た)べる人(ひと) (the person eating); わからない人(ひと) (the person who doesn't understand)]

あん珍は顔立ちが大変美しく、世の女性たちは一目惚れしてしまうような姿形をしていました。

あん珍 Anchin (the priest's name)
顔立ち looks; features
大変 very
美しく beautiful; handsome
世 world; society
女性たち women; females
世の女性たち the world's women
は as for [topic marker]
一目ぼれ love at first sight
ような appeared to; similar to
姿形 appearance; form [of falling head over heels in love]

ある時、彼は熊野詣でに出かけることにしました。

ある時 one time; once…
彼は as for him, he…
熊野詣で to make a pilgramage to Kumano Shinto Shrine [Anchin intended to train in this area of Wakayama prefecture.]
出かける to leave
ことにしました was decided upon [~ni shimasu means to decide upon… You can use this at a Japanese restaurant: *tenpura ni shimasu*. I'll have the tempura.]

旅の途中、泊めてもらった家には「清姫」という可愛らしい娘がいました。

旅 trip; travel
の途中 during; in the midst of
泊めてもらった家 the house that let him stay
には as for in (the house)

清姫 Kiyohime (the young girl's name) [姫 (princess) is part of her name but she isn't necessarily a princess. Some versions have her name just as Kiyo.]
という such a
可愛らしい lovely; sweet
娘 daughter
いました there was

この清姫は、あん珍を一目見るなり気に入ってしまい、毎日毎日、あん珍に「お嫁さんにしてください。」と頼みました。

この this
一目見る at first glance; take one look at [We've already seen 一目ぼれ (love at first sight); *hito me* means "at a glance"]
なり immediately
気に入った was pleased; liked; suited
しまい *[shows completeness and sometimes regret]*
毎日毎日 every day; all the time [repeated for emphasis]
あん珍に to Anchin
お嫁さん bride; marry into
にしてください   please take
と *[quotation marker]*
頼みました asked; requested

あん珍は、「修行の身ですから、結婚するわけには行きません。」と断りましたが、

修行 training; study; discipline
修行の身 (his) focus is with training; his body is reserved for training [Here, he means his body is reserved for Buddhist training and not able to be given to her for marriage; 学生の身 (focusing on studying [literally, a student's body])]
ですから therefore; so...
結婚する to marry
わけには行きません impossible to do [even if desired]
断りました declined; refused; rejected
が but; however

あまりにもしつこいので、とうとう「それでは熊野詣での帰りに、またこの家に立ち寄ることにします。」と約束してしまいました。

あまりにも excessive; too much
しつこい insistent; obstinate; tenacious
ので therefore; because
とうとう finally; at last
それでは well, then... [This is often used when parting: それではまたね (Well, then. See you again.)]
熊野詣で to make a pilgrimage to Kumano Shrine
の帰りに on return
また again
この家に to this house
立ち寄る stop by; return; visit
ことにします to decide
と約束してしまいました so he promised [The しまいました implies a kind of regret. His actions would later prove deadly.]

清姫は、この言葉を信じて何日も何日も待っていましたが、あん珍はさっぱり帰ってきません。ついに、清姫は自分で探しに行くことにしました。

この言葉 this word; these words
を [direct object marker]
信じて believed
何日も何日も for many days [The repetition is for emphasis. 何日 by itself means 1) what day or 2) how many days.]
待っていましたが (she) waited, but...
さっぱり not in the least; completely
帰ってきません didn't return
ついに finally; at last
自分で by oneself; by herself
探しに行く went to look for [The に shows intent and gives the reason (探し) for going (行く)]
ことにしました decided to (go)

途中で何人もの人に尋ねると、
「ああ、あの人ならあなたの村とは反対の方へ行ってしまったよ。」

途中で while (searching); during
何人も everyone; many people
人に to people
尋ねると asked and... [The と means "upon doing this (asking), the following happened"]
ああ ah
あの人 that person; that man
なら if (you mean that person)
あなたの村 your village
とは and; in comparison to
反対 opposite
方 direction
反対の方へ toward the opposite direction
行ってしまった left
よ [sentence ender showing certainty or emphasis]

清姫はあん珍に騙されたと知り、急いで追いかけ始めました。

に騙された tricked; played the fool [騙す damasu–to trick; 騙される to be tricked]
と知り upon understanding
急いで quickly
追いかけ始めました began to chase after [追いかける *oikakeru* (to chase; to run after) + 始める *hajimeru* (to begin)]

追いかけているうちに、清姫の足は擦り切れ、何やら尻尾のようなものが体の後ろから伸びてきました。

追いかけているうちに while pursuing
清姫の足 Kiyohime's feet
擦り切れ to wear out; to be reduced; shrink away [Her legs were wearing away and shrinking (as she became the dragon) 擦る (to rub; to scrub) + 切る *kiru* (to cut; to wear out)]
何やら something; for some reason
尻尾のようなもの some thing like a tail
体 body
後ろ behind
体の後ろから from behind her body
伸びてきました lengthened; stretched

目はらんらんとひかり、ハアハアと息をする口は大きく横に裂けてきました。なんと、清姫は大蛇に変わってしまったのです。

目 eye
らんらんと glaringly; flamingly
ひかり light; shine; glitter
ハアハアと [effect of panting]
息をする to breathe
口 mouth
ハアハアと息をする口 the mouth that made panting sounds when breathing
大きく to become larger
横に on the side
裂けてきました split; tear
なんと how!; what!
大蛇 large serpent; large snake
に変わってしまった changed into
のです the fact is…[explanatory ender; のです or のだ or the abbreviated forms んです or んだ are used when giving or asking for an explanation for something. The reason is that… The fact is that…]

「あん珍様、あん珍様！」と呼ばれて、後ろを振り返ったあん珍は仰天しました。

あん珍様 Anchin (polite)
と呼ばれて was being called
後ろ behind
振り返った turned behind; look behind
仰天しました was amazed; was horrified

大蛇が自分の名前を呼びながら、ハアハアと息を弾ませて追いかけてくるのです。大慌てで逃げ出しました。

自分の名前 one's (his) own name
呼びながら while calling
ハアハアと effect of something panting or gasping]
息 breath
弾ませて bursting with (panting breath)
追いかけてくる was chasing [The くる is an auxiliary verb that indicates something is starting or happening: やっと分かってきました *yatto wakatte kimashita* ((I) finally (came to) understood.)]
のです the fact is… [explanatory ender]
大慌てで in great haste; in a mad rush
逃げ出しました ran away [逃げる *nigeru* (to run away; escape) + 出す *dasu* (to get out; to exit)]

「あん珍様、なぜ逃げるのですか。おのれ、裏切ったな。私のところに帰ってくると言ったのは、嘘だったのか。」

なぜ why
逃げる run away
のですか [ender asking for explanation]
おのれ You! [used as an accusation; Japanese has many pronouns. This one, like 貴様 *kisama*, is used as a kind of fighting word: You! You betrayed me...]
裏切った betrayed
な [sentence ender indicating emotion or emphasis]
私のところに to me; to my place
帰ってくる return back
と言った (you) said
のは as for that
嘘 lie
だった was
のか wasn't it? [ender that questions the preceding statement]

あん珍は、大慌てで「道成寺」というお寺に逃げ込み、助けを請いました。

大慌てで with great haste
道成寺 Dōjōji [name of a temple in Wakayama]

すると、お寺の人たちは、「お寺の鐘の中にお入りなさい。」と言って、お寺の鐘を下ろし、そこにあん珍を隠しました。

という such a
お寺に to temple
逃げ込み escape into; flee to [逃げる *nigeru* (to escape; to flee) + 込む *komu* (to go into)]
助け help; rescue
請いました asked; solicited
すると upon doing so; and then
お寺の人たち the people of the temple
鐘 bell [large hanging bell]
中 inside
鐘の中に to (go) inside the bell
お入りなさい please enter [polite]
と言って said thus
下ろし lowering; dropping
そこに in there
隠しました hid

大蛇は、お寺にやってくると、その鐘を見つけて、その鐘に巻きつきました。

大蛇 big snake; serpent
お寺に to the temple
やってくると finally came and then
その鐘 that bell
見つけて found
巻きつきました wrapped around (that bell)

そして、口から火を吐きなが
ら、その鐘を燃やし尽くしてしまい
ました。鐘の中に隠れていたあん珍
は、焼け死んでしまいました。

そして and then
口から from mouth
火 fire
吐きながら while spitting out
燃やし尽くして burned all up [燃やす *moyasu* (to burn) + 尽くす (completely; exhaust; to the end)]
鐘の中に within the bell
隠れていた (that) had hid
焼け死んで burned to death [焼く *yaku* (to burn; to scorch) + 死ぬ *shinu* (to die)]
しまいました [shows completion and regret]

そして、大蛇はそのあと川に飛び込んで死んでしまったということです。
　おしまい。

そして and then
大蛇 big snake; serpent
そのあと after that
川に into a river
飛び込んで jump in; leap in
死んで died
しまった [shows completion and often regret]
ということです that's that [This is a way to wrap up the story; "...and that's how it was"]
おしまい the end

あん陳と清姫
Anchin and Kiyohime in Japanese

　今から千年ほど昔のこと。あるところに「あん珍」という名の若い山伏がいました。山伏というのは、山に住んで仏教の修行をする人です。あん珍は顔立ちが大変美しく、世の女性たちは一目惚れしてしまうような姿形をしていました。

　ある時、彼は熊野詣でに出かけることにしました。旅の途中、泊めてもらった家には「清姫」という可愛らしい娘がいました。この清姫は、あん珍を一目見るなり気に入ってしまい、毎日毎日、あん珍に「お嫁さんにしてください。」と頼みました。あん珍は、「修行の身ですか

ら、結婚するわけには行きません。」と断りましたが、あまりにもしつこいので、とうとう「それでは熊野詣での帰りに、またこの家に立ち寄ることにします。」と約束してしまいました。

　清姫は、この言葉を信じて何日も何日も待っていましたが、あん珍はさっぱり帰ってきません。ついに、清姫は自分で探しに行くことにしました。

　途中で何人もの人に尋ねると、「ああ、あの人ならあなたの村とは反対の方へ行ってしまったよ。」清姫はあん珍に騙されたと知り、急いで追いかけ始めました。

　追いかけているうちに、清姫の足は擦り切れ、何やら尻尾のような

ものが体の後ろから伸びてきました。目はらんらんとひかり、ハアハアと息をする口は大きく横に裂けてきました。なんと、清姫は大蛇に変わってしまったのです。

「あん珍様、あん珍様！」と呼ばれて、後ろを振り返ったあん珍は仰天しました。大蛇が自分の名前を呼びながら、ハアハアと息を弾ませて追いかけてくるのです。大慌てで逃げ出しました。

「あん珍様、なぜ逃げるのですか。おのれ、裏切ったな。私のところに帰ってくると言ったのは、嘘だったのか。」

あん珍は、大慌てで「道成寺」というお寺に逃げ込み、助けを請いました。

すると、お寺の人たちは、「お寺の鐘の中にお入りなさい。」と言って、お寺の鐘を下ろし、そこにあん珍を隠しました。

大蛇は、お寺にやってくると、その鐘を見つけて、その鐘に巻きつきました。そして、口から火を吐きながら、その鐘を燃やし尽くしてしまいました。鐘の中に隠れていたあん珍は、焼け死んでしまいました。

そして、大蛇はそのあと川に飛び込んで死んでしまったということです。

おしまい。

Story Two:
あん陳と清姫
(ちん) (きよひめ)

Anchin and Kiyohime in English

This happened about a thousand years ago. In a certain place, there lived a young mountain priest named Anchin. A mountain priest is a Buddhist monk in training who lives in the mountains.

This Anchin had a very lovely face and it seemed all the world's women would fall madly in love with him.

One day, he decided to go study at Kumano. While on the trip there, he stopped at a certain house and met a lovely daughter by the name of Kiyohime. She liked him at first glance. Every day she begged Anchin to "take me for your bride." But Anchin declined by saying, "I'm concentrating on my training and I therefore cannot get married."

But she was so persistent, he finally promised, "Well then, when I get back from Kumano, I will come to this house again."

Kiyohime believed those words and waited every day. However, Anchin never returned. Finally, Kiyohime went to look for him herself.

While searching, she asked many people.

"If you mean *that* person, he is going in the opposite direction of your village."

When Kiyohime realized she had been deceived, she immediately took off. While on the search, her legs began to shrink and somehow something like a tail stretched out behind her. Her eyes glittered and panting breath came out of her mouth which was itself enlarging.

Kiyohime had changed into a large serpent.

"Anchin! Anchin!"

Turned to look back, Anchin was terrified by what he saw. A large serpent was calling his name and panting loudly while chasing him. Hurriedly, he ran away.

"Anchin! Why do you run from me? You betrayed me," she said. "'I will come back to you'—that was a lie, wasn't it?"

Anchin hurriedly ran to Dōjōji Temple. Running inside, he yelled, "Help!"

Then the men of the temple said, "Hide under the large bell." They lowered the large bell and there Anchin hid.

The large serpent finally came to the temple and found the bell. She wrapped around the bell and then fire came out of her mouth. That bell melted completely and Anchin burned to death.

Then the large serpent jumped in the river and drowned.

The end.

Japanese Reader Collection Volume 6: Yuki Onna

Kanji in Focus

The following are a few of the most important kanji found in this book. The underlined reading is probably the most used. If there is a . that means what comes before the dot is in the kanji and what goes after the dot follows the kanji in hiragana.

朝
- **READINGS** チョウ; <u>あさ</u>
- **MEANING** Morning
- **EXAMPLE** 朝寝坊(あさねぼう) oversleeping; late riser

小
- **READINGS** ショウ; <u>ちい.さい</u>; こ; お; さ-
- **MEANING** little; small
- **EXAMPLE** 小学(しょうがく) elementary school

大
- **READINGS** チョウ; ダイ; タイ; おお-; <u>おお.きい</u>; おお.いに
- **MEANING** big; large
- **EXAMPLE** 大学(だいがく) university

蛇
- **READINGS** ジャ; ダ; イ; ヤ; <u>へび</u>
- **MEANING** snake; serpent
- **EXAMPLE** 黒蛇(くろへび) black snake

朝
- **READINGS** チョウ; <u>あさ</u>
- **MEANING** Morning
- **EXAMPLE** 朝寝坊(あさねぼう) oversleeping; late riser

二

READINGS: ふた.; ふ.; ふう; <u>に</u>
MEANING: two
EXAMPLE: 二月(にがつ) February

人

READINGS: ジン; ニン; <u>ひと</u>; -り; -と
MEANING: person
EXAMPLE: 日本人(にほんじん) Japanese person

吹

READINGS: スイ; <u>ふ.く</u>
MEANING: blow; breathe; emit
EXAMPLE: 吹雪(ふぶき) blizzard; snowstorm

雪

READINGS: セツ; <u>ゆき</u>
MEANING: snow
EXAMPLE: 大雪(おおゆき) heavy snow

方

READINGS: <u>ホウ</u>; かた; -がた
MEANING: direction; person; alternative
EXAMPLE: 一方的(いっぽうてき) one-sided; unilateral

日

- **READINGS**: ニチ; ジツ; <u>ひ</u>; -び; -か
- **MEANING**: day; sun
- **EXAMPLE**: 毎日(まいにち) every day

火

- **READINGS**: カ; <u>ひ</u>; -び; ほ-
- **MEANING**: fire
- **EXAMPLE**: 火山(かざん) volcano

一

- **READINGS**: <u>イチ</u>; イツ; ひと; ひと.つ
- **MEANING**: one
- **EXAMPLE**: 一回(いっかい) once; one time

晩

- **READINGS**: バン
- **MEANING**: nightfall; night
- **EXAMPLE**: 晩御飯(ばんごはん) supper; dinner

目

- **READINGS**: モク; ボク; <u>め</u>; ま
- **MEANING**: eye; look
- **EXAMPLE**: 目的(もくてき) purpose; goal; aim

見

- **READINGS**: ケン; <u>み</u>.る; み.える; み.せる
- **MEANING**: see; idea
- **EXAMPLE**: 意[いけん]見 opinion; view; comment

息

- **READINGS**: ソク; <u>いき</u>
- **MEANING**: breath; respiration
- **EXAMPLE**: ため息[いき] sigh

今

- **READINGS**: コン; キン; <u>いま</u>
- **MEANING**: now
- **EXAMPLE**: 今月[こんげつ] this month

夜

- **READINGS**: ヤ; よ; <u>よる</u>
- **MEANING**: night; evening
- **EXAMPLE**: 夜中[よなか] midnight; middle of the night

着

- **READINGS**: チャク; ジャク; <u>き</u>.る; -ぎ; き.せる; -き.せ; つ.く; つ.ける
- **MEANING**: wear (clothing); arrive
- **EXAMPLE**: 水着[みずき] swimsuits; bathing suit

物
- **READINGS**: ブツ; モツ; <u>もの</u>
- **MEANING**: thing; object; matter
- **EXAMPLE**: 動物(どうぶつ) animal

清
- **READINGS**: <u>セイ</u>; ショウ; シン; きよ.い; きよ.まる; きよ.める
- **MEANING**: pure; purify; cleanse
- **EXAMPLE**: 清潔(せいけつ) clean; hygienic; sanitary

姫
- **READINGS**: チキ; <u>ひめ</u>
- **MEANING**: princess
- **EXAMPLE**: 一姫二太郎(いちひめにたろう) [Japanese saying] It's best to have a baby girl first, then a boy.

風
- **READINGS**: フウ; フ; <u>かぜ</u>; かざ
- **MEANING**: wind; air; style; manner
- **EXAMPLE**: 風景(ふうけい) scenery

雪
- **READINGS**: セツ; <u>ゆき</u>
- **MEANING**: snow
- **EXAMPLE**: 初雪(はつゆき) first snow (of the season)

女

READINGS ジョ; ニョ; ニョウ; <u>おんな</u>; め
MEANING woman; female
EXAMPLE 男女(だんじょ) women and men

DOWNLOAD LINK

Please go to this website to download the MP3s for both stories: (There is an exclusive *free* **gift on kanji** waiting there too.)

http://japanesereaders.com/1049

Thank you for purchasing and reading this book! To contact the authors, please email them at help@thejapanshop.com. See also the wide selection of materials for learning Japanese at www.TheJapanShop.com and the free site for learning Japanese at www.thejapanesepage.com.

Made in the USA
Las Vegas, NV
12 January 2023